the Name Above Every Name

Study Guide

KENNETH COPELAND

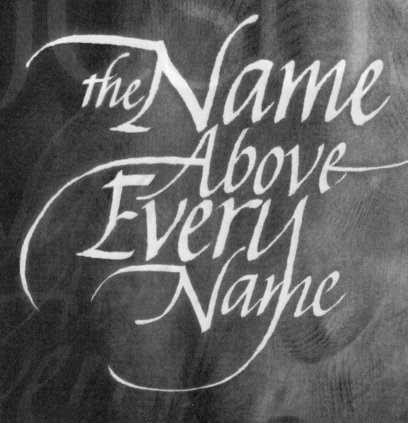

the Name
Above
Every
Name

Study Guide

KENNETH
COPELAND
PUBLICATIONS

KENNETH COPELAND

Unless otherwise noted, all scripture is from the *King James Version* of the Bible.

Jesus—The Name Above Every Name

ISBN-10 1-57562-691-8   30-0725
ISBN-13 978-1-57562-691-8

18 17 16 15 14 13   9 8 7 6 5 4

© 1983 International Church of the Word of Faith Inc. now known as Eagle Mountain International Church Inc. aka Kenneth Copeland Publications.

Kenneth Copeland Publications
Fort Worth, TX 76192-0001

For more information about Kenneth Copeland Ministries, visit kcm.org or call 1-800-600-7395 (U.S. only) or +1-817-852-6000.

Printed in the United States of America. All rights reserved under International Copyright Law. No part of this book may be reproduced or transmitted in any form or by any means, electronic or mechanical, including photocopying, recording, or by any information storage and retrieval system, without the written permission of the publisher.

1

*"Wherefore God also
hath highly exalted him,
and given him a name which
is above every name: That at
the name of Jesus every knee
should bow, of things in heaven,
and things in earth, and
things under the earth."*

Philippians 2:9-10

The Name of Jesus is above every name. Jesus has
given the Church His Name and all the power and
authority it carries.

CD ONE
Jesus—The Name Above Every Name

God Always Responds
to the Name of His Son

You have a right to use the Name of Jesus.
You're part of the family!

You Have Been Given Power of Attorney to Use the Name of Jesus

FOCUS: "And these signs shall follow them that believe; In my name…" (Mark 16:17).

Every believer should have a revelation of the power that's available to him in the Name of Jesus. Proverbs 18:10 says, "The name of the Lord is a strong tower: the righteous runneth into it, and is safe."

In Acts 3, Peter used the Name of Jesus and a lame man received his healing. This authority was not given just to the apostles or the early Church. Jesus gave the entire Church the authority to use His Name. "Of whom the whole family in heaven and earth is named" (Ephesians 3:15).

The commandment given to the Church in 1 John 3:23 is not only to love one another but to believe on the Name of Jesus as well. Mark 16:17 says, "And these signs shall follow them that believe…." The Name of Jesus releases the power of God to meet every person's need and set the captives free.

> *Jesus gave the entire Church the authority to use His Name.*

It is vital to see that words are important. Jesus said to speak to things—things like mountains, sycamore trees and the sea. He told the sea, "Peace, be still" (Mark 4:39).

Words are filled with power. When something is called by a particular name repetitively, it is enforcing and confirming that name. People do this in the negative all the time and don't think anything about it. But Jesus said by our words we are justified and by our words we are condemned (Matthew 12:37). As believers, we should be vitally aware of our words and speak blessing instead of cursing.

Now, in John 17:22, Jesus was praying for us when He said, "And the glory which thou gavest me I have given them; that they may be one, even as we are one." The same glory and honor God displayed when He said of Jesus, "This is my beloved Son" (Matthew 3:17), He has given to believers as His beloved children.

Jesus has given the Church His Name and all the power and authority it carries. When His Name is released from the mouth of a believer in faith, Satan has to flee. He recognizes the Name of Jesus. He knows the power it carries.

> *The Name of Jesus releases the power of God.*

God said, "They shall call his name Emmanuel, which being interpreted is, God with us" (Matthew 1:23). The name *Jesus* means "Savior." This does not mean salvation alone. It means the One who gave the new birth, made man free, poured out righteousness and injected eternal life—the God kind of life—into the spirit of man.

Philippians 2:9-10 says, "Wherefore God also hath highly exalted him, and given him a name which is above every name: That at the name of Jesus every knee should bow, of things in heaven, and things in earth, and things under the earth." God knew how much power and authority would have to be in the Name of Jesus for it to cover the entire spectrum of Satan's existence. The Name of Jesus is above every name. His Name is above all sickness, poverty, worry and any other evil work of Satan. ❧

When we use the Name of Jesus, we're using the authority we have in Him.

Now Begin Enjoying It

Ephesians 1:21 says Jesus is "far above all principality, and power, and might, and dominion, and every name that is named...." He is the head, the Church is His Body and all things are under His feet. Since we are in Him, all things are under our feet!

A revelation of this wonderful Name and speaking it with your mouth will cause you to exercise your position as a joint heir with Jesus Christ.

C D 1 Outlined

I. The Church has been given the Name of Jesus and all
the power and authority it carries
   A. The Name of the Lord is a strong tower (Proverbs 18:10)
   B. Peter used the power in the Name of Jesus (Acts 3)
   C. The authority was not just given to apostles and
      the early Church
   D. The authority of His Name was given to the
      entire Church

II. The commandment given to the Church is twofold
(1 John 3:23)
   A. Love one another
   B. Believe on the Name of Jesus (Mark 16:15-18)

III. The greatness of His Name is described in the
Scriptures (Isaiah 9:6; Matthew 1:23)

IV. The high Name of Jesus is above every name
(Philippians 2:9-10; Ephesians 1:21)

Study Questions

(1) Explain why the Church has the right to use the Name of Jesus.

_____

_____

_____

_____

(2) What is the commandment given to the Church and how is it fulfilled?

_____

_____

_____

(3) Why do words play such an important role? _____

_____

_____

_____

_____

*(4) What does the word **Savior** mean when referring to the Name of Jesus?*

_____

_____

_____

(5) Why did God put so much power in the Name of Jesus? _____

_____

_____

_____

_____

Study Notes

_____
_____
_____
_____
_____
_____
_____
_____
_____
_____
_____
_____
_____
_____
_____
_____
_____
_____
_____
_____
_____
_____
_____

"And this is his commandment, That we should believe on the name of his Son Jesus Christ, and love one another, as he gave us commandment."
1 John 3:23

2

"The name of the Lord is a strong tower: the righteous runneth into it, and is safe."

Proverbs 18:10

The Name of the Lord lifts the
believer high above evil.

CD TWO

Reality of the Authority of the Name of Jesus

Practice Making the
Devil Tremble

*J*esus' prayer is that we be kept from evil…in
the Name of the Lord.

In the Name of Jesus, the Believer Is Above the Circumstances

FOCUS: "Far above all principality, and power, and might, and dominion, and every name that is named, not only in this world, but also in that which is to come" (Ephesians 1:21).

We read in Proverbs 18:10, "The name of the Lord is a strong tower: the righteous runneth into it, and is safe." Other translations say the righteous are lifted high above evil. This scripture directly relates to Ephesians 1:21 and Philippians 2:9. The Name of Jesus is high above every name that is named. When the believer uses it, it lifts him above the circumstances.

Now, in Matthew 18:18 Jesus said, "Whatsoever ye shall bind on earth shall be bound in heaven: and whatsoever ye shall loose on earth shall be loosed in heaven." To understand this scripture you need to know there are three different heavens. There is the heaven that is the atmosphere of this planet, there is the stellar heaven which is called outer space, and there is the heaven which is the dwelling place of God.

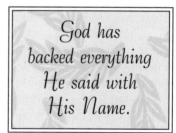

God has backed everything He said with His Name.

There is not anything in the heaven where God dwells that needs binding or loosing. No evil work is present there.

But the high places of this earth are those heavenly places where the principalities, powers and wicked spirits operate. Jesus was explaining that when you bind the work of the devil on earth, it is bound in those heavenly places.

The Body of Christ has been given the Name of Jesus and The Word of God to take authority over the evil dominating the heavenly realms.

Words carry spiritual power. They are alive. They activate the forces in the heavenly realms. They are weapons in the world of the spirit. Faith is operated by words. But it is difficult to use this power to any degree of proficiency if there is a lack of discipline where the tongue is concerned.

> *You are a joint heir with Jesus and have the same ability as Jesus.*

James 3 says a man who bridles his tongue can bridle his body. Verse 6 says the tongue sets on fire the course of nature. The tongue is vital to activating faith and the power of God in the life of the believer.

The shield of faith is what quenches all the fiery darts of the wicked (Ephesians 6:16). Satan tries to influence the thoughts in the believer's mind, so ultimately he can control the believer's tongue. But through the supernatural power of God, the tongue can be controlled by the believer. The Name of Jesus and The Word of God keep the tongue operating for good purposes. So speak The Word of faith in Jesus' Name (Romans 10:8).

It is important to recognize how closely Jesus connected The Word of God and the Name of God. In John 17:6, He said to the Father, "I have manifested thy name…." In Hebrew, God's Name is *El Shaddai*. It means "the Supreme, Almighty, Most High, Healer, Provider, Deliverer, God of gods, Father of spirits." Whatever you need, that's what He calls Himself. He says in His Word, "I am the Almighty God…" (Genesis 17:1). If you need healing, He says, "I am the Lord that healeth thee" (Exodus 15:26). There's nothing you can need that His Name doesn't cover. His Name is all in all—and above all.

In John 17:12, Jesus said of His disciples, "I kept them in thy name." He was always telling them who God really is. He said, "He that hath seen me hath seen the Father…. the Father that dwelleth in me, he doeth the works" (John 14:9-10). Jesus manifested all that God is. He brought life, healing and deliverance to the people.

Jesus was acting on the covenant that God had made with Abraham. A covenant cannot be made without a name to back it. God has backed everything He said with His Name. Historically, that is why a man's word and his name are so closely related. If a man's name is good, his word is good.

You are a joint heir with Jesus and have the same ability as Jesus. You can manifest the Name of God like He did. Through faith in His Name, you have been commissioned to take healing—spirit, soul and body—to a sick and dying world.

Now Begin Enjoying It

Don't wait until your back is against the wall with problems to use the Name of Jesus. Colossians 3:17 says, "Whatsoever ye do in word or deed, do all in the name of the Lord Jesus, giving thanks to God and the Father by him."

The Name of Jesus truly is your strong tower. Put it to work in your life, and it will lift you high above the circumstances you face every day.

CD 2 Outlined

I. The Name of Jesus is high above every other name (Ephesians 1:21; Philippians 2:9)

II. By using the Name of Jesus, the righteous are lifted high above evil (Proverbs 18:10)

III. Believers have authority in the heavenly realms by using the Name of Jesus and The Word of God

IV. Jesus connected The Word of God and the Name of God (John 17:6, 12)

V. Jesus manifested the Name of God
   A. He was acting on the covenant
   B. The believer can manifest the Name of God like Jesus did to bring healing and deliverance

Study Questions

(1) Explain Matthew 18:18. _____
_____
_____
_____

(2) What is the importance of words? _____
_____
_____
_____
_____

(3) How is the tongue controlled? _____
_____
_____
_____
_____

*(4) What does the Name **El Shaddai** mean?* _____
_____
_____
_____
_____

(5) How does Jesus' ministry on earth apply to you personally? _____
_____
_____
_____

Study Notes

"Wherefore God also hath highly exalted him, and given
him a name which is above every name...."
Philippians 2:9

3

*"*Being made so much better than the angels, as he hath by inheritance obtained a more excellent name than they.*"*

Hebrews 1:4

Jesus' great Name was inherited...but that's not all.

CD THREE
The Greatness of the Name of Jesus

You've Been Given
Power of Attorney

You are a joint heir with Christ.
His Name is your name.

In the Name of Jesus, You Have Authority in the Earth

FOCUS: "In my name shall they cast out devils…"
(Mark 16:17).

The greatness of the Name of Jesus is threefold:

1. Hebrews 1:4 says Jesus received the greatness of His Name by inheritance.
To understand how much power is behind an inherited name, it must be measured by the resources of the person from whom the name is inherited. To measure the power behind the Name of Jesus would be to measure the power of Almighty God. Ephesians 3:15 says the whole family of God has been named after Jesus and the Father.

2. Jesus' Name was conferred upon Him.
God exalted Him and gave Him a Name above every name. Hebrews 1:8 says, "But unto the Son he saith, Thy throne, O God, is for ever and ever…."

3. Jesus achieved the greatness of His Name by conquest.
Colossians 2:15 says, "And having spoiled principalities and powers, he made a show of them openly, triumphing over them in it." He went into the pit of hell and suffered there for three days and nights for the penalty of Adam's high treason. Jesus was the substitutionary sacrifice. He paid the price. He was the first to ever be reborn from sin to the righteousness of God. After He defeated all the powers of hell, He laid His blood on the mercy seat. He had the keys of death and hell. Satan was rendered helpless in every realm.

What did Jesus do with the Name that was given to Him? He conferred it upon the Body of Christ.

In Matthew 28:18-19, Jesus said, "All power is given unto me in heaven and in earth. Go ye therefore...." He has given the Church the authority to use His Name to bring salvation, healing and deliverance to the world. He is the head and the Church is His Body. The head and the body are not separate. They work together. They have the same name. We have been given the power of attorney to use His Name, in His stead.

Heaven has it recorded that when Jesus went to the cross, you went to the cross. He was your substitutionary sacrifice. Heaven declares that His Name is your name and that you were crucified with Him. Galatians 2:20 says, "I am crucified with Christ: nevertheless I live; yet not I, but Christ liveth in me: and the life which I now live in the flesh I live by the faith of the Son of God, who loved me, and gave himself for me."

> *His Name is your name.*

When Jesus rose from the dead, you rose from the dead. You are seated with Him, far above Satan and all of his cohorts (Ephesians 2:6). You have the full armor of God, the Name of Jesus and The Word of God. Satan cannot tell the difference between you and Jesus.

Now Begin Enjoying It

Choose to walk in the victory Jesus provided through His death, burial and resurrection. You were there with Him; now reign with Him. You have victory now in the matchless Name of Jesus.

C D 3 Outlined

I. The greatness of Jesus' Name is threefold
   A. Jesus inherited the greatness of His Name (Hebrews 1:4)
   B. Jesus' Name was conferred upon Him (Hebrews 1:8)
   C. Jesus achieved the greatness of His Name by
      conquest (Colossians 2:15)

II. Jesus gave His Name to the Body of Christ
    (Matthew 28:18-19)
    A. We take His Name to the world
    B. We have the power of attorney to use His Name

III. His Name is the believer's name (Galatians 2:20)
     A. The believer identifies with His death, burial
        and resurrection
     B. We now reign with Him in victory

Study Questions

1) Explain how Jesus inherited His Name. _____
_____
_____
_____
_____

(2) How was His Name conferred upon Him? _____
_____
_____
_____

(3) What did Jesus do to obtain His Name by conquest? _____
_____
_____
_____
_____

(4) What kind of power and authority has the Church been given because
of His Name? _____
_____
_____
_____

(5) How does this Name apply to you personally? _____
_____
_____
_____

Study Notes

"And hath raised us up together, and made us sit together
in heavenly places in Christ Jesus."
Ephesians 2:6

4

*"And his [Jesus']
name through faith
in his name hath made
this man strong...."*

Acts 3:16

Faith is the power source for the privileges
that are ours in the Name of Jesus.

CD FOUR
Exercising Your Rights to the Name

It's Yours...Now Use It!

God expects you to live by faith.

Jesus Will Develop Your Faith in His Name by His Word

FOCUS: "So then faith cometh by hearing, and hearing by the word of God" (Romans 10:17).

The Word shows us the importance of having faith in the Name of Jesus and the power it makes available. In Acts 3, Peter and John encountered a lame man asking for alms at the gate of the temple. Peter told the man, "Look on us." He was not drawing the man's attention away from Jesus and onto them. Peter was drawing his attention to Jesus *in* them.

The man looked at them *expecting to receive something*. Peter, using his faith, said, "Silver and gold have I none; but such as I have give I thee: In the name of Jesus Christ of Nazareth rise up and walk" (verse 6). Verse 16 says, "And his name through faith in his name hath made this man strong...." Healing was accomplished because Peter knew his position in Christ and used that powerful Name in faith.

There are two different words used in the New Testament for power. There is dynamic power to energize and the power of attorney, or authority. The word *power* in Acts 1:8, "But ye shall receive power, after that the Holy Ghost is come upon you," is translated *dynamite* in the English language. The original Greek translates it as "power, dynamic in its working." But the power referred to in John 1:11 is *authority:* "But as many as received him, to them gave he power to become the sons of God, even to them that believe on his name."

These two powers work together when using the Name of Jesus. It was the Name of Jesus and faith in His Name that healed the lame man. This was a demonstration of the power of authority and the power, dynamic in its working.

Every believer has been given the right and authority to use the Name of Jesus. But without faith there is no power to operate these privileges.

It is important to operate by faith in every area of life. Romans 1:17 says, "The just shall live by faith." The principles of faith are the same whether using the Name of Jesus, receiving healing, salvation, prosperity or anything from God. The sacrifice of Jesus at Calvary and His resurrection from the dead covered it all. And the whole system works by faith. It is the power source that causes all these things to function.

On the negative side, when Adam bowed his knee to Satan, it covered every aspect of life. It brought spiritual death to man which, in turn, affected his mind and body. A curse came upon all mankind.

> **Faith is the power source.**

But the work God did through the death, burial and resurrection of Jesus was far more powerful than what Satan did in Adam. Romans 5:17 says, "For if by one man's offence death reigned by one; much more they which receive abundance of grace and the gift of righteousness shall reign in life by one, Jesus Christ."

Operating by faith in the Name of Jesus gives you the ability to overcome and reign in life.

Faith is a fruit of the re-created human spirit. It can be developed and put into operation by using the following steps as a guideline:

1. Put The Word first place. Whatever The Word says about the Name of Jesus, stand on it.

2. Meditate on The Word. Allow the Holy Spirit to reveal The Word of God to you concerning the Name of Jesus.

3. Act on The Word. Put actions to what The Word says to do.

4. Decide to live by faith. Make a quality decision to use the Name of Jesus in every area of life.

5. Decide to live by love. Use the Name of Jesus where other people are concerned.

6. Receive Jesus as the developer of your faith. Romans 10:17 says, "So then faith cometh by hearing, and hearing by the word of God." Jesus will develop your faith by His Word.

Now Begin Enjoying It

Practice using the Name of Jesus. Meditate on God's Word day and night so it becomes a part of you. In a time of pressure, you will act on The Word inside you, in faith. By understanding the authority in Jesus' Name and your right to use His Name, you will overcome.

CD 4 Outlined

I. Using the Name of Jesus in faith produces results
   A. In Acts 3, a lame man was healed through Peter
      1. The man's attention was drawn to Jesus in Peter
      2. He expected to receive
      3. Faith in Jesus' Name made him whole

II. The authority of Jesus' Name is available but must
    be received

III. Two kinds of power are spoken of in the New Testament
   A. The power mentioned in Acts 1:8 refers to a
      dynamic, energizing power
   B. Power of attorney or of authority is what we have, as
      children of God

IV. Faith is the power source for our privileges
   A. Apply the six steps for results
   B. Practice using Jesus' Name in faith

Study Questions

1) Why did Peter want the lame man's attention? _____

_____

_____

_____

_____

(2) Why was the lame man healed? _____

_____

_____

_____

(3) Why should faith be exercised in every area of life? _____

_____

_____

_____

_____

(4) How do you give The Word first place? _____

_____

_____

_____

(5) Explain the importance of practicing the Name of Jesus. _____

_____

_____

_____

Study Notes

"So then faith cometh by hearing, and
hearing by the Word of God."
Romans 10:17

5

"**Put** on the whole armour of **God**....
Above all, taking
the shield of faith."

Ephesians 6:11, 16

Faith is your most important piece of armor.

CD FIVE
faith in the Name of Jesus

You Control the Essential
Ingredient to Success

God's Word must be mixed
with your faith.

Act on The Word by Faith in Jesus' Name…and Receive

FOCUS: "And his [Jesus'] name through faith in his name hath made this man strong…yea, the faith which is by him hath given him this perfect soundness…" (Acts 3:16-17).

When Jesus ascended, He told His disciples to do everything in His Name and by His Word. Faith in Jesus and His Name is available to every born-again believer.

Faith is the most important piece of the armor of God. In Ephesians 6:16, Paul says, "Above all, taking the shield of faith…."
It is through faith that every piece of armor functions. It is a spiritual law that works when put into operation. Faith functions the same way for salvation as it does for healing and every other benefit of the plan of redemption. But you have to get in The Word and develop faith in an area to be able to receive. The steps to the development of faith and receiving from God in any area are always the same.

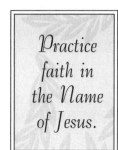

Practice faith in the Name of Jesus.

Let's look again at some of the steps to developing your faith in the Name of Jesus:

1. Put The Word concerning the Name of Jesus first. Make a quality decision not to compromise. Trials and tribulations will not develop faith. The Word of God, activated in faith, will keep you from giving in to tests and trials.

The storms of life did not defeat the man whose house was built on sand; it was his foundation that defeated him (Matthew 7:24-27). He heard The Word but did not put it first. When the storms came, his house fell. The storms also came to the man whose house was built on the solid foundation of rock, but they could not destroy it. He was established. His house did not fall.

> When you activate The Word in faith, it works.

2. Meditate on The Word. Take time to meditate on scriptures pertaining to the Name of Jesus. To meditate is to chew, mutter, attend to, declare and imagine. See yourself using His Name for the deliverance of others. When you take time to meditate on God's Word, the Holy Spirit will have the opportunity to reveal the power and authority vested in Jesus' Name to you. His Name will become a reality to you.

3. Act on The Word. After you have made the decision to put The Word first and have taken time to meditate on it, then act on it. The Word will become reality. When you lay hands on the sick in the Name of Jesus, they will recover (Mark 16:18). God's Word is true and when you activate it in faith, it will work.

4. Make a decision to live by faith. Practice faith in the Name of Jesus. If you are developing faith for healing, make the decision to be whole. If you are developing faith in righteousness, find out what The Word says about righteousness and make the decision to walk in the reality of your right-standing with God. No matter what your feelings or your body says, God's Word is true. Circumstances and feelings are temporary and subject to change, but The Word of God is forever.

5. Make the decision to live the life of love. Practice love and use the Name of Jesus to love others. Bring your own feelings in line with The Word. Lay hands on someone who is in need and pray in the Name of Jesus. It is an opportunity for the love of God to operate.

Love is not a feeling, Love is a Person (1 John 4:8). Act on what Love has said, not your feelings. For instance, when John the Baptist was beheaded, Jesus did not retaliate in the natural realm. He retaliated in the spirit realm. He chose God's way. He healed the sick. ໕

The believer has a position of authority in Christ. Every member of the Body of Christ has been given power through the Name of Jesus.

Now Begin Enjoying It

You can use the Name of Jesus because the moment your spirit was re-created, His Name became yours. Develop faith in that Name and you will see results when you put it to work.

CD 5 Outlined

  I. Faith in Jesus and His Name is available to every believer

 II. There has to be faith in His Name for there to be results

III. Faith is the most important piece of armor (Ephesians 6:16; Romans 14:23)

IV. Put faith into operation by using the following guidelines:
   - A. Put The Word first
   - B. Meditate on The Word
   - C. Act on The Word
   - D. Decide to live by faith
   - E. Decide to live by love

Study Questions

(1) Why is the shield of faith the most important piece of armor? _____

_____

_____

_____

_____

(2) What happened to the man who built his house on the sand? _____

_____

_____

_____

(3) Explain how the Name of Jesus becomes reality to you. _____

_____

_____

_____

_____

(4) When do you act on The Word? _____

_____

_____

_____

(5) How can you practice love in your surroundings? _____

_____

_____

_____

Study Notes

"Above all, taking the shield of faith, wherewith ye shall be
able to quench all the fiery darts of the wicked."
Ephesians 6:16

6

"And whatsoever we ask, we receive of him, because we keep his commandments, and do those things that are pleasing in his sight. And this is his commandment, That we should believe on the name of his Son Jesus Christ, and love one another...."

1 John 3:22-23

Believing on the Name of Jesus is a command....
So is loving one another.

CD SIX

Developing Faith in the Name of Jesus

Love people enough to use
your faith on their behalf.
That's what Jesus would do.

"Whatsoever ye shall
ask [demand] in my name,
that will I do…."
John 14:13

Develop Your Faith So You'll Be Ready to Act…in Jesus' Name!

FOCUS: "Go ye into all the world…. Lay hands on the sick, and they shall recover" (Mark 16:15, 18).

First John 3:22 says, "And whatsoever we ask, we receive of him, because we keep his commandments, and do those things that are pleasing in his sight." The commandment given to the Church is to love one another and to believe on the Name of Jesus (verse 23). In Mark 16:15-18, Jesus gave the commandments to use His Name and set people free. He was telling believers to lay hands on the sick and cast out devils. This is how the love of God is revealed to others.

Develop faith in the Name of Jesus. Then when someone needs prayer, you will be ready because you have allowed the Name of Jesus to become a reality to you.

His Name carries authority in every realm. To "drink any deadly thing" and "take up serpents" literally means you can walk into any kind of serpent-infested domain and come away unharmed. The Name of Jesus will spoil and plunder Satan's household and bring his strongholds down.

> *Jesus' Name carries authority in every realm.*

Review three of the steps that will help you develop faith in the Name of Jesus:

1. Put God's Word first. Faith in the Name of Jesus is allowing The Word of God concerning that Name to be the final authority. When The Word has first place, you will respond to it rather than the circumstances—no matter what they are. You must decide to stand on The Word with the Name of Jesus and apply that power so Satan's attack will be stopped. Allow The Word of God to be the center of your life. Make it your No.1 priority.

2. Meditate on The Word. Take time to think about The Word concerning the Name of Jesus. One suggestion is to record the scriptures concerning His Name and play them over and over. Things will begin to be revealed to you that you may have missed previously.

Another suggestion is to write the scriptures down on index cards and keep them where you will see them. The more you meditate on them, the stronger the image will become in your mind. The eyes of your understanding will be enlightened and you will actually see yourself as God sees you. Meditation builds the capacity for faith and you will then activate that Word.

3. Live by faith and practice love. Make a point to surround people with the love of God, particularly those who have mistreated you. This is not done in the natural realm but in the supernatural realm by faith. Forgiveness is an act of your will. It is not done through feelings. It is done by faith. Ephesians 4:32 says that we are to forgive one another, even as God for Christ's sake has forgiven us. Use the Name of Jesus and bring your emotions in line with God's Word.

There are two different ways to use the Name of Jesus. One is to pray to the Father in the Name of Jesus and receive whatever is asked (John 16:23). The other one is the right to make demands in this natural world (John 14:13). You can make demands of your body in the Name of Jesus. Peter made demands on the man's body in Acts 3, when he said, "In the name of Jesus Christ of Nazareth rise up and walk." He was not talking to God, but the man's body. ༺᪥

*Using the Name of Jesus is
a quality decision from which
there is no retreat.*

Now Begin Enjoying It

Exercise your authority because of who you are in Christ. Colossians 3:17 says, "And whatsoever ye do in word or deed, do all in the name of the Lord Jesus, giving thanks to God and the Father by him."

CD 6 Outlined

I. Keep the commandments (1 John 3:22-23)
   A. Love one another
   B. Believe on the Name of Jesus (Mark 16:15-18)

II. Use His Name on behalf of others

III. The Name of Jesus can dominate any realm

IV. Practice the steps to developing faith in His Name

V. There are two ways to use the Name of Jesus
   A. Pray to the Father; receive whatever you ask
      (John 16:23)
   B. Use Jesus' Name to make demands in the natural
      world (John 14:13)

$Study\ Questions$

(1) What is the commandment given to the Church? _____

_____

_____

_____

_____

(2) How do you surround people with the love of God? _____

_____

_____

_____

3) Explain why forgiveness cannot be based on feelings. _____

_____

_____

_____

_____

(4) Explain the difference between the two ways Jesus' Name can be used.

_____

_____

_____

(5) How do you develop faith in the Name of Jesus? _____

_____

_____

_____

Study Notes

"And whatsoever ye shall ask in my name, that will I do,
that the father may be glorified in the Son."
John 14:13

Prayer for Salvation and Baptism in the Holy Spirit

Heavenly Father, I come to You in the Name of Jesus. Your Word says, "Whosoever shall call on the name of the Lord shall be saved" (Acts 2:21). I am calling on You. I pray and ask Jesus to come into my heart and be Lord over my life according to Romans 10:9-10: "If thou shalt confess with thy mouth the Lord Jesus, and shalt believe in thine heart that God hath raised him from the dead, thou shalt be saved. For with the heart man believeth unto righteousness; and with the mouth confession is made unto salvation." I do that now. I confess that Jesus is Lord, and I believe in my heart that God raised Him from the dead.

I am now reborn! I am a Christian—a child of Almighty God! I am saved! You also said in Your Word, "If ye then, being evil, know how to give good gifts unto your children: HOW MUCH MORE shall your heavenly Father give the Holy Spirit to them that ask him?" (Luke 11:13). I'm also asking You to fill me with the Holy Spirit. Holy Spirit, rise up within me as I praise God. I fully expect to speak with other tongues as You give me the utterance (Acts 2:4). In Jesus' Name. Amen!

Begin to praise God for filling you with the Holy Spirit. Speak those words and syllables you receive—not in your own language, but the language given to you by the Holy Spirit. You have to use your own voice. God will not force you to speak. Don't be concerned with how it sounds. It is a heavenly language!

Continue with the blessing God has given you and pray in the spirit every day.

You are a born-again, Spirit-filled believer. You'll never be the same!

Find a good church that boldly preaches God's Word and obeys it. Become part of a church family who will love and care for you as you love and care for them.

We need to be connected to each other. It increases our strength in God. It's God's plan for us.

Make it a habit to watch the *Believer's Voice of Victory* television broadcast and become a doer of the Word, who is blessed in his doing (James 1:22-25).

About the Author

Kenneth Copeland is co-founder and president of Kenneth Copeland Ministries in Fort Worth, Texas, and best-selling author of books that include *How to Discipline Your Flesh* and *Honor—Walking in Honesty, Truth and Integrity.*

Since 1967, Kenneth has been a minister of the gospel of Christ and teacher of God's Word. He is also the artist on award-winning albums such as his Grammy-nominated *Only the Redeemed, In His Presence, He Is Jehovah, Just a Closer Walk* and his most recently released *Big Band Gospel* album. He also co-stars as the character Wichita Slim in the children's adventure videos *The Gunslinger, Covenant Rider* and the movie *The Treasure of Eagle Mountain,* and as Daniel Lyon in the Commander Kellie and the Superkids™ videos *Armor of Light* and *Judgment: The Trial of Commander Kellie.* Kenneth also co-stars as a Hispanic godfather in the 2009 movie *The Rally.*

With the help of offices and staff in the United States, Canada, England, Australia, South Africa, Ukraine and Singapore, Kenneth is fulfilling his vision to boldly preach the uncompromised WORD of God from the top of this world, to the bottom, and all the way around. His ministry reaches millions of people worldwide through daily and Sunday TV broadcasts, magazines, teaching audios and videos, conventions and campaigns, and the World Wide Web.

Learn more about Kenneth Copeland Ministries by visiting our website at **kcm.org**

When The LORD first spoke to Kenneth and Gloria Copeland about starting the *Believer's Voice of Victory* magazine...

He said: *This is your seed. Give it to everyone who ever responds to your ministry, and don't ever allow anyone to pay for a subscription!*

For more than 40 years, it has been the joy of Kenneth Copeland Ministries to bring the good news to believers. Readers enjoy teaching from ministers who write from lives of living contact with God, and testimonies from believers experiencing victory through God's Word in their everyday lives.

Today, the *BVOV* magazine is mailed monthly, bringing encouragement and blessing to believers around the world. Many even use it as a ministry tool, passing it on to others who desire to know Jesus and grow in their faith!

Request your FREE subscription to the
Believer's Voice of Victory **magazine today!**

Go to **freevictory.com** to subscribe online, or call us at
1-800-600-7395 (U.S. only) or **+1-817-852-6000**.

We're Here for You!®

Your growth in God's WORD and victory in Jesus are at the very center of our hearts. In every way God has equipped us, we will help you deal with the issues facing you, so you can be the **victorious overcomer** He has planned for you to be.

The mission of Kenneth Copeland Ministries is about all of us growing and going together. Our prayer is that you will take full advantage of all The LORD has given us to share with you.

Wherever you are in the world, you can watch the *Believer's Voice of Victory* broadcast on television (check your local listings), the Internet at kcm.org or on our digital Roku channel.

Our website, **kcm.org,** gives you access to every resource we've developed for your victory. And, you can find contact information for our international offices in Africa, Asia, Australia, Canada, Europe, Ukraine and our headquarters in the United States.

Each office is staffed with devoted men and women, ready to serve and pray with you. You can contact the worldwide office nearest you for assistance, and you can call us for prayer at our U.S. number, +1-817-852-6000, 24 hours every day!

We encourage you to connect with us often and let us be part of your everyday walk of faith!

Jesus Is LORD!

Kenneth & Gloria Copeland

Kenneth and Gloria Copeland